KLAUS W REICHEL

A Journey to Awareness

Contents

1

Preface

As the solar system moves closer to the centre of our galaxy, our planet is moving to a higher frequency.

The world is changing, and if we don't change with it, we will be left behind.

The knowledge that was acquired years ago isn't enough to navigate our new reality.

This book only scratches the surface of ancient and up to date information. My second book which goes into more depth on these topics is available.

The acquisition of knowledge is a wonderful thing, and those who are seekers of it will reap the rewards. To those who seek knowledge, something different will be given to each.

Discernment is one of the most important factors in your journey. Read the information in this booklet and see what resonates with you.

2

The Way Back

Do you pursue knowledge? Creation is full of mystery and wonder, and this roadmap has been made for you to navigate it. Ancient knowledge has been lost over the centuries and in some cases has been hidden from view to protect the public from itself. As time goes on, more information is released as more people deal with the science that used to be classed as fantasy.

For a meaningful life in these times, it pays to examine not only the common sciences, but others as well.

Besides our digital devices, we all own a state-of-the-art bio computer. What we don't have is the user manual. A lot of people self sabotage themselves and don't even know it. It's similar to leaving your home computer on and letting your cat walk over the keyboard. Some of the programs that are running in your subconscious can turn you into a real mess. And you are not aware of it. So you continue on your way, not realising that your DNA has been changed - not only your own but also for generations to come.

There is more to this world than you first thought. Here is a summary of knowledge that I have picked up over the years to help you navigate it.

A lot of people have been involved in the training and information that I have collected. They are people who have researched the knowledge and proved it to be true. Some earn their living training people, and most of them contribute some knowledge for free. I have done both and the most joy I have had is in helping others.

Contribution to others is one of the most important things that a person can do. And contributing without expecting any reward is really a good place to be. This is usually followed by some unexpected gift. It can be something that one needs at the time, or that one of your kids require in some way. It's always a surprise to me, how things work. I did a good deed for someone at one time, and had no expectation for any reward. What came back to me was two weeks in an apartment in a tourist area for free.

All of what is written here is what I have learned.

This booklet is for the seeker of truth who is interested in finding out more. I especially invite you young people who will be the keepers of our future. You are the people who will look after climate change, the sciences, health care and generally, humanity.

I was walking through life, oblivious to things out there, when at age 52 I realised there was a lot of reality "under the radar". I ended up going to Egypt, Mexico, Germany and the USA to investigate some of the information that I had acquired to prove it was true for myself. At the time it was just plain fun. In the end I discovered another world of information that, quite frankly, blew me away. Sifting through all the information and finding out that a lot of it is plain lies, I realised that digging for the truth is like gold mining. If you look long and hard enough, gold turns up.

The Tools

If you have ever been in a dodgem car at the carnival, you know this - as you steer and drive the car, above you, high on a rod, is a wheel that connects with the power grid to give the car power. In the same way, our conscious mind is driving what we do and where we go, while our subconscious mind is connected to a similar grid as the car in the example. This grid is called *group consciousness*.

Another analogy is the River of Information. We are all connected. Unfortunately, a lot of us don't know it, because that part of our awareness has been switched off. We have lost the ability to see with our mind, and not just with our eyes.

We are all connected. Our body is our vehicle, our mind is the driver.

To switch awareness back on, training in some alternative bio programming is needed. For the lucky few, this awareness has never left them from birth. You can see it in their eyes, and some kids talk like a 35-year-

4

old. You wonder where that all came from. But that's material enough for another book.

Quantum physics is one science, but in this new age one has to look at all the aspects of this reality, even if some aspects seem a bit unreal or bizarre.

This booklet is not a micro investigation of alternative thinking. It's more of a tap on the shoulder to say... "Look at this". And when you do look at it and Google some things, information will come to you, but you need to be aware of the massive amount of data that will turn up.

The connection with the group consciousness is a bit odd. It doesn't conform to any logical rules. Those who meditate correctly and deeply can access records that are unseen or not documented anywhere. One has to realise that the picture painted by our parents, school and work is not the whole picture. It's not their fault, it's how society is. How to Manifest (change your reality) is not part of our training, but hopefully in the future, it will be.

To connect to group consciousness, if you're at home and want to know what your uncle in England is up to, all you need to do is connect with the Information River, and tap into it. You will be taken immediately to a "video" of what your uncle is doing. This is often known as remote viewing or clairvoyance.

In order to hone this skill, training is usually required. And there are some remote view trainers throughout the world.

Also, if you wish to see the emotional state of another, all you do is put that person in a visual bubble, and you will see their state. It's important not to invade someone's privacy though and also to be aware of one's moral obligations for others privacy. Concern for a loved one or friend is a good reason.

Every healing programme needs training, because it has been for-gotten. We need to be reminded how to get it back. You can start at home with books and videos, but ultimately person to person training is advised.

Note: keep away from social media if possible. The truth rarely lives there.

Your intuition is connected to the River of Information. The river holds past, present and future events. It's hard to get your head around it, but in the end, you realise that the truth does set you free.

The mind does not just live in the brain, it also lives in the cosmos

The mind is not the brain. The mind lives in the brain, and the heart, but also in the cosmos. And possibly in other aspects of reality. Therefore, sometimes the mind goes to places that frighten us. We end up wondering if we are going mad, so we shut down any questions that may arise.

But it's all okay. It's very important to keep one's feet on the ground or they could drift off into a world of fantasy. One of the ways to keep grounded is to walk barefoot on grass or walk into the ocean. That does help. Also a bath in magnesium salts will ground you and stop you from flying into the Wizard of Oz land! I went to a little place near Rockhampton in Australia called Emu Park. A cute little village on the ocean. As I hadn't grounded for quite a while, I decided to walk into the ocean. Well, guess who fell over? I couldn't hold my balance. That was a lesson for me. Don't wait too long to touch the earth after doing some work on yourself or connecting with the Information River. Even dealing with others can unground you, so every now and then get grounded.

There is a lot of talk about spiritual people, crystals and religion. I will keep those down to a minimum as it might be confusing. To go back to the analogy of a dodgem car. You, your spirit, is in the car. The car is your body, so when the car wears out your body doesn't function anymore. Your body is only the vehicle, so it is vital to keep the services up or you will break down.

It doesn't matter if you believe in different lifetimes or not. That's your choice, but inheriting trauma from your parents or grandparents is a fact. If grandma had a traumatic experience that experience went into her cells. It's called cellular memory. As you have kids and they have kids, that trauma is sometimes transferred to the next generation. Unfortunately, the kids have no clue that this has happened, except they do behave a little strangely under different circumstances, but they don't know why. There are several alternative bio programmes that can get rid of this. They are listed at the end of this booklet.

The Programming of Reality

The greatest shock to me was the realisation that what we speak and think can affect our reality. It's a tough wakeup call. Can what I say or think, change the outside of me? Yes and Yes.

If you are forever saying and thinking, "I haven't got enough money" then that's what happens to you. You seem to be always short of cash.

"I'm always sick, I don't think I'll be well ever again". If you keep repeating it over and over again, you will programme your reality to do that. That's a very hard pill to swallow. In some cases external forces that you have no control over affect you which make your life miserable.

A JOURNEY TO AWARENESS

* * *

3

How to Change It

One of the things you can do in that case is say to yourself, "Things will get better; it will change to a better outcome". And continue to say it.

And also make sure you change how you handle the problem. Are you going to die? NO! Will you stop breathing .... NO. Will everything you possess be taken away? ... Maybe. Then get back to, are you going to die?... NO.

Winter won't last forever. It's a slow moving train, but in the end, things will change. The lesson from hardship is how you learn to handle adversity. If you take the analogy that the earth is an oven and you are the bread, then you are going to be put under a lot of heat. But like the dough that becomes a loaf of bread - your transformation will take place, and you will be a wiser person in the end. And in the long run, you will contribute and help others.

If you get rid of fear and anxiety, the world would be a different place

Some of the words that seemed to take away the anxiety in my life were as follows - say them out aloud while you're thinking of what's bugging you.

"Thank you for the lesson...I accept the way I feel!"

Those words seem to take away a lot of the pain and suffering. If it only works for a short time, say it again and again over a few days every time that thought turns up. When you accept the way you feel, the lesson doesn't seem to come around again. It's a funny reality.

Now, if you say to yourself "I have oodles of cash......I don't know what to do with it all", then eventually that's what will be. One thing that does programme reality quickly is the spoken word and emotion. If you put those two together, chances are that it will happen for you. It may take a while if you have been saying negative things to yourself for a long time. In any case ... Stop the negative comments - they won't help at all. Complaining about your life, just gives you more of the same.

The equation that either makes us or destroys us:

Thought/Words/Intension + Emotion = Manifestation (Programming Reality)

You can manifest a new car or a broken leg. The universe doesn't care which. Never say "I need a break!!" You may end up with a broken bone!

There is another aspect of our body that just does not compute to most of us. Somewhere in our body is a *Biological Healing App.* We all have it, and we can all use it. In most of us, it's switched off. Over centuries the information has been lost. The thought that only a doctor can cure you has been deeply embedded in our culture. In some cases doctors are needed of course, and it's important to look at all the information.

Even though we may depend on doctors to an extreme in modern life, you can switch your healing app back on. Belief and emotion switches it on. Some people inadvertently switch it on - it is usually mentioned in the science community as a placebo effect.

Training in a modality (Alternative bio programming) is a quick way to heal yourself. But it also can be done by reading, meditation or listening to others.

If you think that Garfield the cat can cure you... and you totally believe it, you will switch on your Healing App, and it will be sorted. It doesn't matter if it's religious, spiritual, a purple rock or music. If you believe with every cell of your body, you will have the power to change your reality and your health.

The saying "If you don't change anything in your life, then don't expect anything to change!" is so true.

Change your self-speak and your thoughts. Especially self criticism. Don't do it!! It will keep you miserable indefinitely. If people knock you and ridicule you, after they go, and sometimes a long time after they leave, you will continue the ridicule, and will constantly do that to yourself.

A Rabbi I saw on Youtube the other day said, "Don't allow other people to live in your mind rent free!!" It's time to evict that recording you play over and over again. That recording can be damaged by many means.

You can change the recording, or damage the recording so you can't play it. Turn it into a funny story. Turn that guy that so insulted you or upset you into Big Bird, or a squeaky mouse!

Or every time you think of playing that recording, stop yourself and replace it with a pleasant memory. You have about 5 seconds to stop it before it gets locked in for another self sabotage session. I have found myself going to old memories on a number of occasions If I stop them early, ...they're gone. And every time I bring it up, I get rid of it, then the time periods between my trying to play that memory again gets, longer. To the point where I just can't play it. Then the emotional upset won't happen. This can happen for you too.

If someone attacks you verbally, listen but don't let it into your body. It's usually their issue, not yours. So don't take ownership of it. Otherwise, it will upset you - it will cut down your immune system and transfer somewhere into your body. And then you have a problem.

If all these factors affect your reality, it's of utmost importance to be careful with what you put into your body.

Not just diet, but also media, spiritual, what you say and your own thoughts.

Those will all shape your reality.

If you're having trouble changing anything in your life, and it's all too hard, start with your thoughts. Those alone will change things.

If you research things that you haven't been taught, you will see a lot more.

Some Connections You Can Google

Theta Healing Sydney Australia (Mark Anthony)

Theta Healing USA

Body Talk

Balancing the Cortices (Body Talk)

Emotional Freedom Technique (EFT)

Gregg Braden

Bruce Lipton

Joe Espenza

Abraham (Esther Hicks)

Joseph M. Carver, Ph.D., Psychologist (Emotional Memory)

Louise Hay (Hay House)

Theta Healing

With Theta Healing, the basic course can set you back a bit of money. So for a start, just order the book *Basic Theta Healing.* You will get an understanding how powerful your mind is.

It's a bit scary at first. You have no idea how much power you have in your mind. The way you can change your reality by your thoughts may at the start seem ridiculous. Theta Healing does use The Creator (God) for all its actions. If you don't believe in a higher power, this won't work for you. Another good book is:

Biology of Belief - by Dr. Bruce Lipton.

It gives you an understanding of how disease is linked to your belief system and every cell of your body.

But if you have an ailment of any kind, please see a medical practitioner. Once you have seen the information and get some training, there will be fewer trips to the doctor.

You can do or be anyone you want to be

Whatever negative happens in your life, it transfers to somewhere in your body if you don't clear the issue. Find out - research ... research. It will be worth it.

There is a book that links disease with issues. It's called:

The Secret Language of your Body - By Inna Segal

* * *

Fear and stress in your body causes your immune system to withdraw. When you have stress in your life, all your energy is sent to help the foe or run for your life, (the flight or fight response), taking energy away from your immune system. Are you going to run away from that tiger chasing you, or are you going to fight that cold? No contest!

Your cold will have to wait. And your cold can turn into pneumonia.

So the best thing to do for your body is to get rid of the stress it's under. The longer the stress, the bigger the issue. So chill!

After seeing what's happening in the world today, the best thing one can do is be in control of one's own health. Do what needs to be done to stay safe. And also do what needs to be done to keep others safe.

The governments around the world haven't seen anything like the Covid-19 virus before, so most are winging it. What was okay last week is not okay this week.

There is an evolution in research and thinking. There are a lot of plot theories out there. A good trick you can do is ask the question, "Is this real?"

After meditating for a while, you will get a Yes or No answer.

Don't take too much notice of plot theories. All these plot theories are an attempt to rationalise what's happening. They are a fabrication that we must deal with, and do not assist us in any way.

4

Meditation Techniques

There are hundreds of meditation techniques to choose from. It's important to realise that to quiet the mind is no easy task. The best thing I found first up is to imagine you're in a boat on a still lake, surrounded by pine trees. Take as long as you like to set the scene:

As you look around you can see the sand on the shore, the rocks and some birdlife. The water is still and calm is the order of the moment.

And yes...... what happens then is...... I have to pay my electricity tomorrow. I have to meet John at 11am at the hardware store....etc...etc...etc. It takes some practice to stay on that lake. You have to fight off all those automatic thoughts that your sneaky brain wants to throw at you. It's tough - don't be surprised if it takes a while to get your mind quiet.

Also.....kids going Mum...Mum....Mum or Dad...Dad....Dad won't do it for you. Wait till they're all in bed. Or super early in the morning before they get up. Preferably go to the same location every day.

I often wonder why people will get up really early for their boss and job but won't get up for themselves. Meditation is important - it changes everything. I remember I was living alone for a while. I couldn't get my mind quiet and I read this article about candles. So that's how I started.

Light a candle and focus on the flame. The most important thing in the room is the candle - not the car, the partner....food... etc. Keep looking at it. It might take a while but then the candle splits into two. You stop focusing because you're relaxing. And then all sorts of things start happening. You swear that the candle moves but it doesn't really - it's just your visuals going a bit silly. Your brain tries to rationalise it, but it can't.

One major thing happens - you're so focused on that candle that nothing else comes into your consciousness.

That's the first step in getting rid of that pesky brain. It wants to run on automatic. But you say, "NO! I'm setting you to manual override, and I'm focusing on the candle."

After some practice, you won't need the candle. Some of us don't need the candle at all to start. It's all about controlling your brain and not letting it bring up unwanted thoughts every 5 seconds.

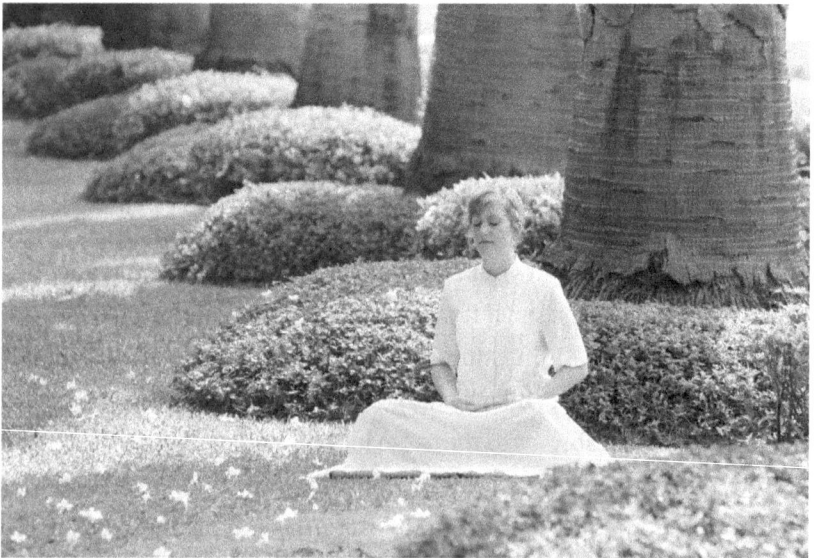

Meditation is the best thing for clearing your mind and helps your body.

Imagination is a big player in meditation. The brain, even though it's a pest, it can be fooled with imagination. If you picture something happening, the brain doesn't know the difference between reality and imagination. If you know how to use this, it's a great tool to use when working on some of your issues.

If you use the analogy of walking down a road to get to your meditation destination, it's going to get very difficult if you have these large boulders (issues you face) all over the road. Also, having a belief that you can't possibly meditate isn't a good start.

Yes, you can! You just need to apply yourself to it. On the net, you can pick up guided meditations where people walk you through a complete meditation. Just pick one that resonates with you.

There is one that's a good starter. If you google Abraham –Esther Hicks, you will find a lot of knowledge there. She has written quite a few books and meditations. She stresses the importance of your having to be in the vortex. The vortex being your inner self. She does convey that she is channeling Spirit, but don't be put off by this – she has some great videos. Look for her guided meditation: *Getting into the Vortex.*

Another good reference is Joe Dispenza. He does have some free videos on meditation on Youtube along with information to change your belief system. The most up to date information is with him.

Brain Function

A lot of things have been said about the brain. Here is a shortcut description. You have the conscious mind that you use every day to operate everything from your iPad to your car. All this takes place in your conscious mind. It's a bit of a shock to find out that this part is used about 5% of the time. The majority of your brain is functioning in the subconscious. It can process information 1000 times faster than the conscious mind and is basically the holder of the programs of teachings, habits and emotional memory. It is a bit of a pest. You may want to change part of your "programming" because your behaviour is causing you or others grief. But because your subconscious is really a bio recorder of everything and it holds your programming, it's nearly impossible to change just by your conscious thoughts. One of the alternative bio programmes like EFT or Theta Healing can help you change the programmes. As your subconscious is a recorder, you can actually record over the old programming.

An example of this is an overweight lady who wants to lose weight. So she diets and gets some of her weight off, and then she hits a wall. The body just does not agree with what she wants. The conscious mind is saying "I want to get thin. I'll look stunning and I'll be a lot healthier as result"

But the subconscious is not so interested in doing that. It knows if she loses weight and looks good, she is going to get hit on by guys. That's ok, but wait, she has already had four bad relationships. Why would she want to look good? It might lead to another bad relationship, so for self preservation the body stops losing weight.

The bad news is, she is not aware that this is happening and continues the diet without much success. And in the end, frustrated, she gives up.

You can circumvent that by re-writing the programme. Something like "It doesn't matter what weight I am, I will attract a warm and loving partner who will only care about me."

Thinking it consciously just won't be enough. You need a modality that can reprogram your subconscious. Hypnotherapy for example can do it.

There is one other slow way – you can repeat the same thing to yourself in a mantra. It takes a lot of repeating; 1000 times at least.

If you walk for exercise, do it while walking every time. It will change your programming eventually.

The following is from Louise Hay from Hay House.

An affirmation you may want to say:

All is well, everything is working out for my highest good. Out of this experience, only good will come and I am safe.

When I first started out I knew nothing. You have to seek and be selective of what you accept as the truth. I usually hear the same thing on numerous occasions before I look at it.

If you look for the truth it will find you. Books are a good place. A lot of books are not published on the net. Going on the net has a lot of pitfalls. The truth is sometimes hidden from you, so you need to cross check, double check, and ask questions of those you trust. Take heed of what you are being told. Messages come from all places, including the ones that don't appear to be a message at all.

I have a couple of examples. Once my car had a flat and the spare was flat. I was so annoyed with myself for not checking the spare. It took me 2 hours to get to a service station, fix the tyre and return. I had a 7 hour trip and was halfway, when at two am, I saw police cars, an ambulance and the rescue squad across the highway.

I stopped and asked if I could help and was told a car had hit a horse. When I asked what time it happened, they told me two hours earlier. That was the exact time I would have been coming through, if I hadn't had that flat tyre delay. Hitting a horse with my then small Toyota would have done me in.

After that, I learned that if I was delayed, it didn't matter. The universe was protecting me.

In the second example, I was in a bank and the guy next to me was talking to the bank teller. He was so annoyed that he didn't check his spare tyre in his car . When he needed it, it was flat. Sound familiar?

That time I took notice, and when I went to the service station to check, it was flat. That was the second time I let the spare go flat. There hasn't been a third time. I always check now.

When you overhear things, ask yourself the question, was that for my benefit? When you accidentally pull the wrong book out of the library...ask again. If you jump onto a website that just came up because you pushed the wrong key, ask again. Was that meant for me?

Messages come from all places and some appear really crazy, but listen anyway.

At one stage I went to a lawyer to enquire on how I should handle my separation from my first wife. I really didn't want to divorce her. I thought it was too much. The lawyer gave me some financial guidance and recommended I get divorced. When he said those words a magpie tapped his beak on the window glass.

My solicitor said, *You see? even the magpie (bird) says to do it.*

I decided to go through with it, and as it turns out, it was the best thing I ever did.

Another story

I was flying to New York on Emirates Airline, and there was a storm there. The pilot tried to land but decided on the last minute to go to Boston instead. The airline put us up at the Hilton for 5 days while the storm passed. An all expenses paid holiday in a 5-star hotel. I met a lot of really good people and was grateful that I was in one piece. At the end of it, I was the last one to leave. The airline representative ordered a limosine to take me back to the airport. I thought, Why did this happen? I'm not sure but it was great. I just said, Thank you, God.

5

Proactive Tools

Dowsing

Dowsing is a very odd thing. It started when people searched for water with a willow stick. It has progressed from there to different systems. You can use steel, copper, crystal and just about anything. One must realise that years ago, they used to burn people at the stake for doing things like this. A lack of knowledge, religious dogma and fear had caused this. But advancements in science have solved a lot of mysteries and questions concerning spiritual technology.

Although some of the mystery has been explained, there is still a void larger than the Grand Canyon that defies explanation.

Dowsing causes various things to happen. To this day, they still don't know why electrons flow when a magnetic field is applied to a copper cable. We just know that it does.

If you hold two L shaped pieces of wire straight out away from you and walk over the top of an underground pipe or electrical service, the wires will move together when you cross over the pipe. Why? We don't know – they just do.

Get a 300mm long (or a 1 foot) piece of string and tie a weight to it, like a crystal, a gold ring, or a steel nut. And let the weight hang there .

You will see after some minutes that the weight swings. If you then say, "Show me yes," it will move differently. And if you say, "Show me no," it will move differently again. This is not some demon moving the weight. It's you, but you're not conscious of it. Once you get a firm yes or no, questions can be asked.

Because your mind is connected to everything, you will get an answer. If nothing happens I would look at getting some training on dowsing. Everyone can do it. You can also clear negative energy in a room with a pendulum, but that's another story.

Remote View

I went to Western Australia to be part of a Remote View class. As most of the class is copyrighted, I can't divulge the method they used for training, but what I can tell you is that the method works. After 3 days of training, I was tested at 78% accurate. Some others were tested at 95% accurate. The tests are quite basic - find the location of X, or describing the contents of a photo hidden from view.

The forum that I enrolled with was quite interesting. A man traveled around Australia, and on his trip, he picked up rocks at different places. He put a number on each of them, and left them at various locations. The exercise for the class was to work out where the location of rock 2334, 2764 and 7665 were.

Surprisingly, the group got a pretty good success rate.

From what I've learned, practicing helps grow neurons in your brain to expand your awareness. As you practice, you get better at it.

I remember taking a photo of the class. The head trainer appeared to have a white cord coming out of his head going up to the ceiling. I thought it was a camera malfunction. I thought it might have been a crack in the brick wall behind him. Then I looked at other photos. The same chord was coming out of his head, and nobody else. It dumbfounded me for a while, until I went back to the analogy of the dodgem car. He was well connected to the River of Knowledge. It was apparent in the photo because he had done remote view for years and his "power" was greatly increased through practice.

It was another confirmation to me regarding the River of Knowledge. We are all connected, but most of us are oblivious to it.

Remote view has been quite successful in finding some missing persons throughout the world.

The more you seek, the more information will come to you.

Muscle Testing

You can ask your body questions and it will answer yes or no. How can that happen? It can't speak, or can it? Your body has muscles, and if you ask a question certain muscles will tighten up, while others loosen. You need another person for this. If you hold one of your arms out straight and let someone else put pressure on your arm, you will see that your arm muscle is tight and will not want to move.

Now make an obviously false statement - if you're a lady, say "I am a man." It is untrue, so immediately your arm becomes weaker. Or if you're a man, say "I am a lady", and the same will happen. Here's something that's interesting to try - do that test, then pick up a mobile phone. Your arm will become weak. That's an indication that mobile phones disrupt your body.

I prefer another version – stand still in one spot and do the test. If it's true, your muscles will tighten up and make you tilt forward. If it's untrue you will sway backwards. Do the man / lady test. If it's in reverse, you are not hydrated enough. Have a glass of water and try again a bit later.

It is best to keep the question topics about your body such as - is this vitamin pill good for me? The standing up method is the best for me, because I can check things in public, without anybody noticing what I'm doing. Otherwise you may be picked up by the men in white coats to take you away. People don't comprehend alternative bio programming, and are in fear of anything that is different.

6

Raising your Vibration

This is a tough one. Everything that is made in the universe has a vibration, including emotions, words, and sounds. The higher the vibration, the more the person is connected to the River of Information.

Angry, miserable people appear to have a low vibration and kind happy people have a higher vibration. And as you get into vibrations, intuition gets better as one scales the vibration tree. Also health-wise, nothing can exist that's bad for you in a high vibration. To get there takes a lot of self analysis though, and some of us are chicken to look in the mirror. All those people in your past that you had arguments with, some are not guilty of starting it. You are. That's a hard one to deal with, but you do get through it eventually. The best thing to increase your vibration is meditation.

The next best thing is the right music. If it affects you emotionally, then it's a winner.

Being conscious of who you are friends with is crucial as well. Your circle of friends is important to your own wellbeing. And sometimes it's best to walk away than keeping a connection going with toxic people. They don't do you any favours.

If you find birds of a feather, seekers of knowledge, that's a good start.

It's important to find groups that you resonate (are switched on) with.

One thing that I'd like to mention is the negative people that may cross your path. If you discover something while seeking knowledge and you want to tell a friend about it, make sure you are considerate regarding their beliefs. If something goes against their beliefs, it's better to keep it to yourself. Also, if you start telling your loved ones what you are researching, they possibly may dump on it. Not because they want you to look stupid, but because they love the person you are, and the last thing they want is for you to change. If you change, they may lose you. It could be anything from a funny look to a screaming match.

Your silence about your own seeking is golden. Sometimes you are so excited to tell another, but it wouldn't turn out well. You don't want to be judged or misunderstood.

When I was doing the Remote View course in Western Australia, I flipped out. How can I draw a picture of a photo that was hidden in a drawer in another room?

I got so enthusiastic, I tried, I really tried to tell some of my friends. They thought I was cracked.

Call out the men in the white coats and drag me away. I must be insane. Later on I realised what that was.

I was staying with a flat mate. His name was Bill, and was a very good guy. But Bill was the biggest skeptic I had ever met. I got into a discussion one day regarding quantum physics. In the end I told him if a UFO landed on his front lawn and little green guys got out of it, he wouldn't believe it. He would believe he was drugged, or hypnotised. I got so frustrated with that situation that I talked to a psychologist friend. It appears, Bill had a problem with fear. That was the underlying issue. That would explain a lot of things to me, and how people react to alternative medicine, alternative realities and quite frankly, as Einstein once said, *spooky action*. It's only because it's not in a textbook or on the news or in a science paper.

When I was learning Theta Healing, I was told that thoughts can change DNA. That was 15 years ago. I was ridiculed by some people and laughed at. Last year the science community proved it without a doubt. I'm glad I stuck with it. Emotion can also change DNA. You have switches that are turned on or off in your DNA. If you have a trauma of some kind, your DNA will alter. Some switches will be turned on and others turned off just like the cat walking across your home computer keyboard. You're not aware of it, but something has changed.

Gratitude

One of the things that one needs to be happy and successful in this life is to be grateful for what one has. Even if it looks like you have nothing and you're miserable. Feeling down and destroyed doesn't give you any advantage at all and it's very hard to get out, once you find yourself in the room of no hope.

And the door appears locked. One way is to use prayer to unlock the door. The other is medication that will take you out of it. It's often been said that if you keep repeating and complaining about your present position, you keep praying for what you don't want. That's very true. If you send it out to the universe, the universe will give you more of the same.

To change that, you must be thankful for your life. In some cases, it's best to be thankful before you even get what you desire. And the funny thing is, when you appreciate what you have, things come to you. It just happens.

What you have is also your body that functions well, your family and your friends. Even your beat up old pickup truck. You don't have to walk, do you? Maybe that's what keeps you alive. If you had a shiny new Ferrari, you may rap yourself around a pole. One doesn't know the motives of the universe.

Silence

It's important to have quiet time. A study quite recently has also proven that being out in nature, or even more explicit, seeing the colour green is good for one's mental wellbeing. It's good just to sit quietly, and you never know what messages may come into you. If none come, that's okay too. If you give your senses a rest, then you give your mind a rest. Nothing may happen while you're in that state. But, when you leave that place of peace and tranquility, you don't get so aggravated and can deal with things more calmly.

Check Your System

It's especially important to get a checkup at least once a year. A simple blood test gives the doctor a lot of information. For the guys, it's so easy to add a PSA test to a blood test. The PSA test gives the doctor an indication that the prostate is ok and you don't have cancer. And don't think it's for the oldies. The other day a 24-year-old died of prostate cancer. Monitoring your cholesterol and blood sugar is also a good idea. As for the ladies, it's important to keep up with the usual tests. It's pretty easy if you catch something early. And one thing that got me testing was not that I was worried to leave this planet. It was more of a case of how my loved ones would deal with me not being here. Look after yourself. It's the only you, that you have.

7

My Revelation

I understand that not everyone in the world has the same reaction or reasoning that I do. We all think we are normal (whatever that may be!)

To have compassion, you must realise that not everything revolves around you and your ideas. Have compassion for people and their problems, and don't judge them.

Most importantly learn that you can gently say no, without anger or resentment.

I must follow my path and take the journey that's right for me.

And shine the light that is within me, onto others.

But most of all, I must find the truth in my surroundings and also within me.

* * *

I received a message once in meditation for those who identify themselves as seekers.

"Your job is to offer a glass of water. That's all you do !" If they accept the water, great, if they don't, that's okay too, but my part of offering the knowledge is done. Sometimes your information is rejected at first. But then, that same person hears exactly the same thing three other times from different places, prompting them to investigate.

If there is something in this booklet that makes life easier for just one person, I celebrate with joy.

8

Some Poetry that was Inspired

The Light

Before we can see the truth in the light,
We must first look at the truth in the mirror,
And see oneself as one really is.
Only then, will a window be opened,
To show you the splendour of creation.

The Anchor

To hold someone tightly in a storm
And brush the fear away from their turbulent skies.
To become serenity and peace,
Is a blessing to behold.
To stand fast amidst adversity,
When all is lost,

To summon the courage,
And find the joy,
To be an Anchor for a friend.

The Garden

Sitting in this garden,
So many miles from home.
I see the raindrops on the leaves,
I see the morning sun transform the night to morning.
Raindrops dance in wonder of every change in light.
Nature composes a symphony for a new day.

So I am drunk on nature.
    All is at peace.
    What is that drop under my eye?
    It is not a raindrop,
    But a tear of joy.

Knowing I am sitting with my brothers and sisters,
    The trees, the flowers, the birds,
    And what is that blowing on my cheek?
    Is it the wind?
    Or is it a memory of old friends and bygone days.
    I can only guess,
    Because –
    The Wind is All I Know.

Links to Healing Modalities

Healing Modalities:
    Theta Healing Australia
    https://thetahealing.net.au/
    Emotional Freedom Technique
    https://eftinternational.org/
    Theta Healing USA
    https://www.thetahealing.com/
    Emotional Freedom Technique USA
    https://www.emofree.com/
    Body Talk System
    https://www.bodytalksystem.com/